NEW YORK
GIANTS

Pat Ryan

CREATIVE C EDUCATION INC.

Published by Creative Education, Inc.
123 S. Broad Street, Mankato, Minnesota 56001

Designed by Rita Marshall

Cover illustration by Lance Hidy Associates

Photos by Allsport USA, Bettmann Archives, Duomo, Focus
On Sports, Sportschrome and Wide World Photos

Library of Congress Cataloging-in-Publication Data

Ryan, Pat.
　New York Giants/Pat Ryan.
　p.　cm.
　ISBN 0-88682-377-3
　1. New York Giants (Football team)—History.　I. Title.
GV956.N4R93　1990
796.332′64′0974921—dc20　　　　　　　90-41259
　　　　　　　　　　　　　　　　　　　　　CIP

A lady overlooks the New York harbor. That lady is the Statue of Liberty. The "Lady of the Harbor" welcomes new families to this country. A plaque on the statue reads, "Give me your tired, your poor, your huddled masses yearning to breathe free."

Not far from the statue is Ellis Island, where millions of immigrants first landed when coming into this country. America has been called the "melting pot" because it brought together people from all over the world. These new residents brought with them many of their old

All-time Giant great Charlie Conerly (#42).

customs. While maintaining their cultural identities, they also embraced all that was American including football, which in time would become an American game.

Millions of immigrants had already come to America by the time the New York Giants football team was founded. Tim Mara, the Giants' first owner, acquired the rights to the team in 1925. Although football was considered only a college game in the early 1900s, Mara and the Giants found loyal fans from the start.

1 9 2 5

Founder Tim Mara bought the Giants' franchise for a mere $500.00.

THE EARLY YEARS

The New York area was very different back in the 1920s when professional football was just getting started. People traveled by streetcar and in Model T automobiles. The game of football was different, too. The athletes had to play both offense and defense. Scores were usually low and the running attack was the biggest part of the game. Leather helmets and high-top shoes were the uniform of the day. And sometimes the teams played four games in eight days. A ticket to a football game was a dollar and the players earned fifty dollars a contest.

As a result of these conditions, football players in the early 1920s had to be extremely tough. Red Badgro, one of the pioneer Giant players, remembers how rough it was. "Dr. March was running the Giants for Tim Mara when I came to them," said Badgro. "I had cut my chin open in practice. I needed eleven stitches to close it up. I just went by his office and he didn't have any of his medical equipment with him, so he got a plain needle and sewing thread out of his drawer and sewed up my chin. He liked football more than the practice of medicine, I believe."

Another tough Giant, Lawrence Taylor (#56).

1 9 4 8

Quarterback Charlie Conerly passed for over 2100 yards during the season.

Despite tough players like Red Badgro the Giants endured some long seasons in the early 1920s. Tim Mara went through three coaches in three years and didn't find a successful leader until he hired Earl Potteiger, who led the team to a record of 11-1-1 in 1927. After Potteiger left in 1930, Mara was again without a coach. Fortunately for the Giants, he found a football scholar right under his nose. Steve Owen, who had played on the championship team in 1927, was willing to coach and play for the New York team. Owen was a student of the game. And Mara, recognizing Owen's potential, gave him a long-term contract. Owen would go on to coach the Giants for the next twenty-three seasons.

Owen's game was defense. He revolutionized defensive strategy with his "umbrella" defense. The alignment featured a six-man front, one linebacker, and four defensive backs. When the quarterback dropped back to pass, two defensive lineman dropped back to form a semicircle secondary, resembling the top of an umbrella. The umbrella was the grandfather of the modern 4-3 defense used today.

Owen ended his coaching career in 1953 after leading the Giants to six divisional titles and two league championships. His 150-100-17 record compiled over twenty-three seasons still stands as one of the finest in pro football history. Owen saw great players come and go in his years as coach. He managed to get the best out of Hall of Famers like quarterback Arnie Herber, defensive back Emlen Tunnell and center Mel Hein. Steve Owen was a football pioneer who eventually joined these players in the Hall of Fame.

GIFFORD AND THE GLORY YEARS

A new Giants' era was ushered in by Owen's replacement, Jim Lee Howell, in 1954. Howell knew what it took to be a good leader, as attested by a roll call of the assistant coaches who worked under him: Vince Lombardi, Tom Landry, Dick Nolan, Alex Webster. Coaches, however, couldn't win games alone. For that Howell needed a star, an impact player. That player turned out to be Frank Gifford.

New York star Frank Gifford made fifty-one pass receptions, gaining over 600 yards.

Gifford had starred at the University of Southern California, where he was a standout running back. Besides his talent the good-looking Gifford was a leader and a player with a winning attitude. "Frank was the body and soul of the team" said coach Howell. "He was the player we went to in the clutch." And most of the time he would come through.

Gifford led the Giants to five division titles in his twelve seasons and scored a team career record seventy-eight touchdowns. In 1956, Gifford scored the final touchdown in a contest against the Bears that made the Giants the NFL champs.

One of Gifford's biggest games, and perhaps one of the biggest games in the history of the NFL, came in 1958. It was a contest which many football historians believe rekindled interest in professional football. It became known as the Yankee Stadium Classic.

On December 28, 1958, the Giants and the Baltimore Colts were playing for the NFL championship. The list of players involved reads like a Who's Who of football; fifteen

The Giants' offense digs in, (pages 10–11).

1 9 6 0

Kyle Rote was the Giants' top receiver, scoring twenty touchdowns.

men who were present that day would eventually be enshrined in the Hall of Fame. The Giants were led by Charlie Conerly at quarterback. The Colts, meanwhile, had Johnny Unitas at quarterback, with Raymond Berry and Lenny Moore as receivers.

Some football purists disagree with the "greatest game" ranking, because it was a rainy day and there were some sloppy plays. There were six lost fumbles, several interceptions, and numerous missed field goals; still, it was football at its most suspenseful.

The Giants were leading 17-14 with three minutes remaining when Johnny Unitas drove seventy-three yards in three plays. Eventually the drive stalled and Lou Michels kicked a field goal which sent the game into sudden death overtime. When play resumed Baltimore quickly drove the ball the length of the field. With the Giants' defense expecting a Unitas pass, Alan Ameche plowed over the goal line from the one for a touchdown. The Colts were the champions, by a score of 23-17.

The Giants' felt dejected but their owner, Tim Mara, was proud of their efforts. "In 1925, we lost to the Bears, but helped save the NFL. Today we lost again, but pro football is the real winner. We may have lost the battle, but we've won the war." Mara died a few weeks later, but the Mara era continued with his sons taking over at the helm.

A second place finish in 1960 marked the end of Jim Lee Howell's coaching career. The young Mara's tried desperately to hire Vince Lombardi of the Green Bay Packers. When he declined, the Maras promoted assistant Allie Sherman to head coach.

Sherman's first player move was a masterful one. With quarterback Charlie Conerly fading, he traded for San

Francisco's Y.A. (Yelberton Abraham) Tittle. The 49ers had felt that the aging Tittle was "too slow." But in 1961 he would lead the Giants to a 10-3-1 finish and be named the league's Most Valuable Player.

Tittle's success with the Giants would continue for three more years. Besides putting up remarkable individual statistics he led the team to three straight conference titles. The only thing they failed to accomplish was winning the National Football League's championship game.

While Tittle led the offense, Sam Huff was the defensive mainstay for New York in the early sixties. Huff was a hero with the Giants' fans for his bone-crunching style of play. He brought linebacking into the spotlight. Sam Huff was responsible for originating some of the terms football uses today including "blitz," "red dog," and "sack." "He was always strong, swift, and was at the right place at the right time," said coach Sherman. But Huff, a favorite of the fans, was traded to the Washington Redskins in 1964. The trade, coupled with Tittle's retirement in 1965, sent the Giants plunging from the top of the NFL.

The departure of the star quarterback and the trade of the aggressive Sam Huff to Washington left holes in both the offense and the defense. Finding players to fill the key positions was not easy. In 1964, the Giants' record fell to 2-12.

1 9 6 3

Quarterback Y. A. Tittle passed for thirty-six touchdowns and over 3100 yards.

TOUGH TIMES IN NEW YORK

Over the next fifteen years, the Giants had the best the league could offer in quarterbacks. Five different head coaches brought in Earl Morrall, Fran Tarkenton, Norm Snead, and Craig Morton. But even with this gallery

Running back Ron Johnson was the club's top rusher with 902 yards.

of greats, the Giants couldn't find the right formula. The defense that had been so important to the Giants in the past was in ruins.

The Giants were in a shambles. The organization tried everything, from personnel changes to changes in surroundings. The Giants played at the Polo Grounds, Yankee Stadium, and even at Yale University. But nothing worked. Many experts believed the Giants would have to totally regroup before they could climb out of the cellar.

Perhaps the lowest point in the Giants' history came in a game against the Philadelphia Eagles in November, 1978. The Giants had a 17-12 lead and the ball on their own twenty-nine-yard line with only 28 seconds remaining in the game. All Joe Pisarcik, the quarterback, had to do was fall on the ball, and the Giants would run out the clock. For some unknown reason the offensive coordinator sent in a play that required a handoff. Pisarcik took the snap, turned, and stuck the ball right into running back Larry Csonka's hip. The ball bounced on the frozen field and Eagle defender Herman Edwards scooped it up and ran in for the winning touchdown. The Giants had managed to snatch defeat from the jaws of victory.

The first big change came in 1979, when George Young was named as the Giants' new general manager. Over the next decade, he would successfully orchestrate several trades and select many draft picks that would lead the Giants back to the top. But Young's first job in New York was to find a head coach.

For that, Young looked west. In the San Diego Charger organization he found an assistant coach named Ray Perkins. He would be the man to lead the Giants into the next decade.

Celebrations were uncommon for New York in the 1970s.

1 9 8 0

Linebacker Brad Van Pelt was named to the Pro Bowl for the fifth consecutive season.

Young's next big move did not occur until 1981. And when it happened many did not think it was that big. Amidst a shower of boos, Young and Perkins made an unknown quarterback from Morehead State College by the name of Phil Simms, their first round draft pick.

Eventually, however, Simms, with the help of veterans like Harry Carson and Brad Van Pelt, became one of the key ingredients to New York's success. But something was still missing. In 1980 a porous defense had allowed opponents 425 points, the second most in the NFL. Monday morning quarterbacks around the country were certain that the Giants would be looking for defensive talent in the next draft; and they were right.

TAYLOR MAKES THE TACKLES

When Lawrence Taylor was a child in Williamsburg, Virginia, he wanted to be a baseball player. However, after watching a few football games, he became more and more interested in that sport. When L.T., as he is called, heard the local Jaycees team was going to play a football game in Pittsburgh, he signed up. He wanted to travel and see the world. The young Taylor had no idea where Pittsburgh was on the map, but he wanted to go there.

The coach, Pete Babcock, said, "Kid, you're going to be a linebacker." That was just fine with Taylor. "I got books out of the school library on linebackers," he recalls. "I read a lot of stuff about Ray Nitschke and Jack Ham and Sam Huff. What I read was how they saw the game, what

16   *Current Giant coach Bill Parcells, (page 17).*

Special teams' star Lee Rouson, (pages 18–19).

While Taylor was gaining all the attention, defensive end George Martin (right) set a Giant record by returning two fumbles for touchdowns.

their feeling was, what their tempo was. I got this concept right then that aside from being smart, a good linebacker was also mean."

After the Jaycees experience the 5-feet-7, 180 pound Taylor found another helpful coach at Lafeyette High School. "Coach Melvin Jones was like a cross between Vince Lombardi and Jesse Jackson," remembers Taylor. "He had all these inspirational sayings plastered all over the walls. One of them really stuck with me." The quote was, "If you can perceive it and believe it, then you can achieve it."

Five years later, as a junior at North Carolina University, Taylor was 6-feet-3 and weighed 230 pounds. He had become one of the strongest and fastest linebackers in college history. Taylor distinguished himself in college as a "big play" man. In play after play, he made game-saving tackles and fumble-producing sacks. In his senior year, one-third of his tackles were behind the line of scrimmage. Most of the pro scouts saw Taylor as the kind of player who could make the transition to the professional ranks with great ease.

As Taylor completed his senior year in college, another change was taking place in New York. Giants' coach Ray Perkins left the team to coach at Alabama. In response, the front office immediately named his assistant, Bill Parcells, as head coach. Several weeks later, the Giants drafted Taylor, and Parcells moved quickly. After Taylor's first week in camp, Parcells turned to an assistant coach and said, "I gotta get this kid into the game."

Linebacker Harry Carson was selected to the All-NFL team for the fifth time.

By the end of his first year in the NFL, Taylor had already made an impact. "L.T. had nine and a half sacks his rookie season and ninety-four solo tackles and he assisted on thirty-nine others," recalled Parcells. "But what he really did was change the way the other teams looked at our defense. He scared them, is what he did." Taylor was everywhere. If a team was going to run or pass against the Giants, they had to get around him first.

Parcells had something to smile about; he knew he finally had a leader on defense who could match his leader on offense, Phil Simms. With Taylor taking care of the defense, Parcells and Simms were working together to take the Giants' offense to the top of the NFL. Simm's greatest strength was his work ethic. He was a working-class quarterback. "The best thing I can say about Phil Simms," said receiver Phil McConkey, "is he's the quarterback every lineman would love."

By 1984, Taylor, Simms, and the Giants were winners once again. They won the NFC wild card playoff spot and

One of Phil Simms' favorite targets, Mark Bavaro.

beat the L. A. Rams 16-13 in the wild card game. Taylor missed Joe Montana too often in the NFC championship game, however, and the 49ers took the title.

The 1980's was a decade of powerful teams, and if the Giants were going to achieve the ultimate goal—playing in the Super Bowl—everyone would have to be in top form. But Lawrence Taylor was not himself in 1985. That year the Giants made it to the playoffs again but lost to another powerhouse, their traditional rivals the Chicago Bears. Worse than the defeat, though, was the news that the rumors about L. T. were true: he was having problems with substance abuse.

Running back Joe Morris rushed for a club record twenty-one touchdowns.

Once again Taylor would have to heed his favorite quote, "If you can perceive it and believe it, then you can achieve it." This time what he needed to achieve was an end to his addiction. Taylor went into treatment for drug abuse.

Bill Parcells waited patiently for Taylor, and when L. T. came back he knew things would be better. "When he came back, I told him to just play football and I'd do the best to take care of everything else. My job—as a coach and as a friend—was to create the best possible environment for him at that point." It must have worked, because 1986 was a super year for New York.

The Giants were on the move. With Phil Simms throwing, Joe Morris running, and Phil McConkey catching and cheerleading, the Giants were piling up victories. They were 10-0 at home and they set all-time attendance records for both home and away games.

The Giants' defense, meanwhile, was the best in the league. Lawrence Taylor was back and he was better than ever. He had twenty and a half sacks, the second highest

Clockwise: Phil Simms, Harry Carson, Joe Morris, Lawrence Taylor.

total in league history, and he was also named the Most Valuable Player in the National Football League. Only one other defensive player, Alan Page, had ever earned this honor.

L. T. was in good company, because his fellow players were also having glorious years. Joe Morris ran for 1,516 yards, breaking his own season record with the Giants. Mark Bavaro caught sixty-six passes for 1,001 yards, both records for a Giant tight end. Raul Allegre, the New York placekicker, didn't miss a field goal from less than forty yards in the last seven games of the season. Behind all of these strong individual performances, the Giants compiled a 14-2 record, tying the Chicago Bears for the best record in the NFL.

1 9 8 6

October 27: Lawrence Taylor recorded three quarterback sacks in a game against Washington.

The team's success continued in the postseason as well. Playoff massacres of San Francisco (49-3) and Washington (17-0) sent the Giants on to Pasadena to meet John Elway and the Denver Broncos for the championship.

The Super Bowl was a Cinderella story for good friends Simms and McConkey. "Conk" would stand up on the bench, during the regular season and wave his towel to get the fans going. Parcells told him to do his towel act before the Super Bowl and it worked. The fans, as a result, got into the game.

Simms, got into the game, too. He completed twenty-two of twenty-five passes, eighty-eight percent, breaking the Super Bowl record. In the second half he completed ten straight passes and broke another record. The Giants beat the Broncos 39-20, and Simms was named MVP. The Giants began talking about a dynasty.

But Pete Rozelle, at the time the commissioner of football, had made it his goal to bring "parity" to the league.

Running back Joe Morris. (pages 26-27).   25

Rozelle and the owners were trying to make the teams more equal by using the draft and drawing up tougher schedules for the top teams. For this reason it was becoming very difficult for teams to repeat as Super Bowl champs.

This fact combined with L. T.'s recurring personal problems, Mark Bavaro's contract holdout, Harry Carson's retirement, and various injuries plagued the Giants throughout 1987 and 1988. Parcells had to make adjustments in his offense and defense if the Giants were to return to the Super Bowl.

1 9 8 9

Quarterback Phil Simms passed for fourteen touchdowns and over 3000 yards.

INTO THE NINETIES

Bill Parcells is forecasting a change in the weather for the Giants in the nineties. He got a preview of what was to come in 1989 with another trip to the playoffs. The Giants earned their playoff berth through hard work. "We don't have the stars we had on the Super Bowl team, guys like Harry Carson, Jim Burt, and George Martin, said Lawrence Taylor. "We have a bunch of guys who are just hard workers, guys who want it." Taylor was referring to players like linebacker Carl Banks and safety Terry Kinard who are taking over the responsibilities of leadership.

The philosophy of the Giants in the nineties will be ball control. "I knew the game was changing," said Parcells. "There are too many multiple defenses nowadays, too many different fronts. You can't run eight different schemes against eight different fronts. It's difficult to practice. You're better off just lining up with your big guys and pounding away. I knew the game would come to this someday, and I started preparing for it."

28

A tough defense continues to be a Giant trademark.

Defensive standout Erik Howard (#74).

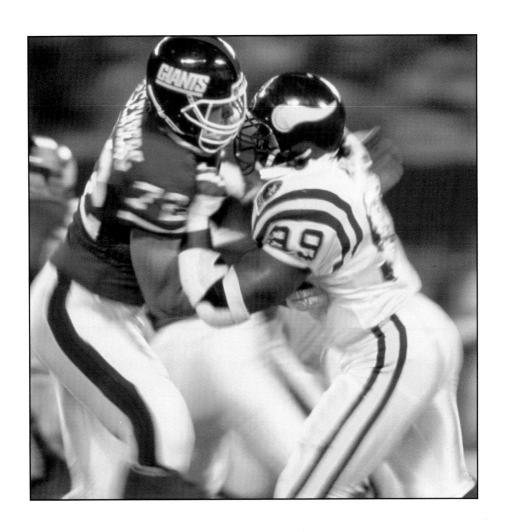

Offensive tackle Doug Riesenberg.

Because of this Parcells' long-range plan centers on the offensive line. The Giants are bulking up for the future. Early-round draft picks Eric Moore, 290 pounds, and Jumbo Elliot, 305 pounds, have been joined by the 330-pound Brian Williams and 288-pound Bob Kratch. The line surge will open up the field for young runners like Dave Meggett, and allow Simms more time for his passing attack. Parcells believes his team is getting better each year, and that his theory of ball control will lead to another Super Bowl spot in the next decade.

Since 1925 the New York fans have been loyal to their team. The Giants are a club steeped in tradition, a tradition of winning. Because of this Parcells, the players, and the fans truly believe that the blue and red will be champions once again in the nineties.